Supporting Your Child's Literacy Learning

A Guide for Parents

BONNIE CAMPBELL HILL

HEINEMANN
Portsmouth, NH

Heinemann
361 Hanover Street
Portsmouth, NH 03801–3912
www.heinemann.com

Offices and agents throughout the world

Library of Congress Cataloging-in-Publication Data
Campbell Hill, Bonnie.
Supporting your child's literacy learning : a guide for parents / Bonnie Campbell Hill.
p. cm.
Standard version ISBN-13: 978-0-325-01272-8 (pbk. : alk. paper)
Standard version ISBN-10: 0-325-01272-5 (pbk. : alk. paper)
1. Language arts (Elementary)—United States. 2. Education, Elementary—Parent participation—United States. I. Title.
LB1576.C3137 2007
372.6—dc22 2007023653

Editor: Leigh Peake
Production: Abigail M. Heim
Typesetter: Gina Poirier Graphic Design
Cover and interior design: Gina Poirier Graphic Design
Manufacturing: Louise Richardson

Printed in the United States of America on acid-free paper
11 10 09 08 VP 2 3 4 5

Acknowledgments

This small booklet evolved over eight years with help from many teachers, university professors, publishers, parents, and students from all around the world. Thank you to Christopher-Gordon for permission to include the descriptors and the family support tips from *Developmental Continuums* (Hill, 2001). They are the seeds from which all this grew.

I want to thank Ann Ebe and Madeleine Maceda Heide, from Hong Kong International School, who created a beautiful early version of this parent handbook. Additionally, Ann, Madeleine, and Carrie and Glenn Ekey helped gather the student writing samples and photographs for the first half of this parent guide. I also want to thank Betsy Suits, who extended the handbook up through the last five stages and collected the writing samples and photographs from the intermediate grades and middle and high school of the International School of Bangkok. I am grateful to all the students and families at the International School of Bangkok and at Hong Kong International School for permission to include their photographs and writing samples in this parent guide.

We appreciate the teachers, families, and students who graciously allowed us to use their photographs on the cover and in the first few pages of this handbook: Troi Graves; David and Conrad Bratz; Celeste, Paulina, and Susan Campbell; Rachel Lee; Mary Freeman Soto and her student and Yvonne and David Freeman (and photo by Julie Farias Photography); Bruce Hill; Florence Campbell and Keith Bolling; Megan Sloan and her class; Anne Klein and Valerie Brayman; and Jake, Toby, and Matthew Mills. Finally, a heartfelt thanks to Leigh Peake and Abby Heim and the team at Heinemann for enthusiastically supporting this venture and creating a very professional document for parents.

The generosity of these many people from all around the world made this project possible and reflects my deep belief that sharing and collaboration enriches all our lives.

Introduction

When each of my three children was born, I turned to my parents, siblings, and other relatives, eager for advice about how to care for my babies. I exchanged ideas with friends and diligently read baby books that outlined the developmental milestones for my children's first years. However, as they started kindergarten and I packed their peanut butter sandwiches in brand-new lunch boxes, put them on their first yellow school buses, and waved good-bye, my heart was filled with a tinge of anxiety alongside all my hopes and dreams. Had I done all I could to prepare them for school? What could I expect as they embarked on their new adventures in school? What I wanted was a book, like those baby books, that would outline their path for literacy development and describe the literacy milestones I should expect as they moved through school. Like many other parents, I wanted answers to two heartfelt questions in terms of my children's literacy:

> How is my child doing as a reader and writer?
> What can I do to help?

We all lead busy lives, so the goal of this book is to provide a short, accessible answer to those two questions. In the next four pages, you will find:

- a brief summary of research about learning to read and write
- a description of how literacy is taught in many schools
- an explanation of reading and writing standards and
- a description of how readers and writers develop along a literacy continuum.

The rest of the booklet then presents, at each of ten continuum stages, samples of reading and writing along with two or three suggestions of things you can do to support your child's reading and writing at home. Of course, this book alone is not enough! I hope you will also communicate with your child's teacher. He or she can provide additional suggestions specific to your child's strengths, needs, and interests. Children blossom when they are nourished as readers and writers both at school and at home. I hope you'll find this book to be a useful tool as you support and celebrate your child's literacy learning.

What Does Research Say About Learning to Read and Write?

- Literacy develops within the framework of real-life activities in order to "get things done." Children learn best at home and at school when they are reading and writing for real purposes and audiences. For instance, writing a letter to a friend who moved away or to an author about a well-loved book is far more engaging than filling out a worksheet because there are a real purpose and audience, and maybe even a letter back!

- Deeper learning occurs when children are actively involved. This means that when children are using invented spelling, they are actively constructing an understanding of how English works rather than just memorizing rules. By sometimes letting your children figure out an unknown word when they read and asking questions after you finish a story, you'll help them become active, and therefore stronger, readers.

- The goals and expectations for young children's achievement in reading and writing should be developmentally appropriate—challenging but achievable. It's important not to push kids into reading books that are too hard. Children need lots of opportunities to write and lots of practice reading "just right" books so they can consolidate the new skills they are learning.

- The role of adults who are supportive, interested, and engaged is critical. Teachers and parents provide "scaffolding" by giving just enough help that children can try new skills as they become more and more independent over time.

- Reading and writing acquisition is best conceptualized as a developmental continuum. However, although there are common patterns, *children learn at their own rate in their own way.* In school, teachers have a variety of ways to assess children's progress in reading and writing in order to help them move forward with their next steps as learners. Your child's teacher can let you know what you can do to help support your child's literacy development at home.

- The best gift you can give your child is to read aloud every day. Research shows that the most important support for children's eventual reading success is reading aloud to them. Don't stop reading aloud when students can read on their own! You can model fluency, expression, and a love of reading, which will support the reading your child is doing at school.

- Encourage your child to read independently at home. The amount of reading students do outside of school has a direct, positive correlation to reading achievement.

How Is Literacy Taught in School?

When I helped my son learn to ride a bike, he learned first by watching me, then by having me run alongside him, holding onto his bicycle seat. As he became more confident, I gradually let go for short bits of time as he wobbled about on his own and found his balance. Eventually he experienced the exhilaration that comes with flying down the hill alone. After that, all he needed was practice with increasingly challenging hills and distances.

Teachers do the same thing as they help students learn to read and write. They read *to* students on a daily basis. They also read *with* students during shared and guided reading, with the whole class, and in small groups. Students talk about the books they read with friends in literature circle discussions and during individual conferences with the teacher. Students also need plenty of time to read on their own each day, both at school and at home. And, finally, they need practice over time with increasingly challenging texts. A similar structure occurs for teaching writing. In the chart below, you can see the basic components of the kind of balanced literacy program you will find in many elementary classrooms.

balanced literacy

READING

Reading Aloud
The teacher reads aloud to the whole class or small groups. A carefully selected body of children's literature is used; the collection contains a variety of genres and represents our diverse society. Favorite texts, selected for special features, are reread many times.

Shared Reading
Using an enlarged text that all children can see, the teacher involves children in reading a text together. The process often includes reading big books, poems, songs, and student writing.

Guided Reading
The teacher works with small groups of readers who have similar reading skills. The teacher selects and introduces new books and supports children reading the whole text to themselves, making teaching points before, during, and after the reading.

Independent Reading
Children read on their own or with partners from a wide range of materials, including a special collection at their reading level.

WRITING

Modeled Writing
The teacher models his or her own writing using a think-aloud process.

Shared and Interactive Writing
The teacher and the children compose messages and stories together. The teacher can serve as a scribe or use a shared-pen technique that involves children in the writing.

Guided Writing
Children engage in writing a variety of texts. The teacher guides the process and provides instruction through minilessons and individual conferences.

Independent Writing
Children write their own pieces. These may include stories, informational or persuasive pieces, response to literature, and poetry.

Word Study
Woven through the activities in this framework, teachers have opportunities to help children notice and use letters and words; knowledge and vocabulary is further fostered through minilessons, activities, and the use of charts and word walls.

Adapted from Fountas, Irene, C., and Gay Su Pinnell. 1996. *Guided Reading: Good First Reading for All Children.* Portsmouth, NH: Heinemann, 22–23.

What Are the Standards for Reading and Writing?

You've probably heard a great deal in the last few years about standards. Schools are working hard to articulate clear goals and expectations for teaching and learning in all areas of the curriculum. Checking students' learning against standards is like taking my children to the doctor for a wellness check each September. I want to make sure my kids are meeting the normal expectations for height and weight and, if not, what I should do.

Although standards may vary slightly in different states and countries, most K–8 Language Arts curriculum documents include literacy standards that look very much like the ones in the following chart. As parents, it's important to remember three things:

1. Attitude is a critical part of learning to read and write. Our most important job as parents is that of cheerleader.
2. We need to focus on what children are trying to communicate in writing *before* addressing spelling and grammar.
3. Reading is more than just sounding out words (decoding). Reading is about making meaning. Comprehension is a vital aspect of learning to read.

READING STANDARDS

Reading Strategies
Students understand and use different skills and strategies to read.

Types of Texts/Genres
Students read different genres and materials for a variety of purposes.

Oral Reading
Students read aloud with fluency and expression.

Comprehension and Response
Students understand the meaning of what is read and respond in a variety of ways.

Reading Attitude and Self-Evaluation
Students read for information, understanding, and enjoyment. They evaluate their own progress and set their own reading goals.

WRITING STANDARDS

Writing Strategies (Content/Traits)
Students write clearly and effectively, using effective organization, word choice, sentence fluency, and voice.

Types of Text/Genres
Students write in a variety of forms and genres for different audiences and purposes.

Writing Process
Students understand and use the steps of the writing process (prewriting, drafting, revising, editing, and publishing).

Mechanics and Conventions
Students explore language usage and apply conventions within the context of their writing.

Writing Attitude and Self-Evaluation
Students analyze and evaluate the effectiveness of written work and set writing goals.

What Are the Stages of Reading and Writing Development?

How Can I Help My Child?

My oldest son took his first steps at 12 months, my daughter at 10 months, and my youngest child at 14 months, yet all of them are walking today! In the same way, not all children learn to read or write at exactly the same time. There's a predictable, developmental sequence of stages in literacy based on the typical "normal" range of children's reading and writing. In the following pages of this handbook, you will find descriptions of the ten stages of reading and writing development. The "ballpark" for growth is indicated by the overlapping age ranges for each continuum stage. The reading and writing continuums are like a roadmap showing where students have been and where they are going. The stages are like road signs along the way (see p. 9).

It is important to remember that reading and writing development take time. Young children need lots of varied experiences with reading and writing to grow as literacy learners. Children will be at different stages at different times depending on many factors. If English is not your child's first language, he or she will go through the same stages, but at a slower rate as they transfer skills from their native language into English. It's important, however, to keep speaking, reading, and writing with your child in your home language to support cognitive growth and vocabulary development.

As you read through the descriptions of each continuum stage, look at the writing samples and the types of books children typically read at each stage and see if you can identify your child's stage for reading and writing. Each page includes a "Parent Tips" section where you will find a few ideas about how to support your child's literacy development at home. Try to provide as many authentic opportunities as you can for engaging in literacy at home and help your child find books to match his or her interests. Together with your child's teacher, you can help your child become a competent and enthusiastic lifelong reader and writer.

The Reading/Writing Continuum

Childhood Is a Journey . . .

Not a Race

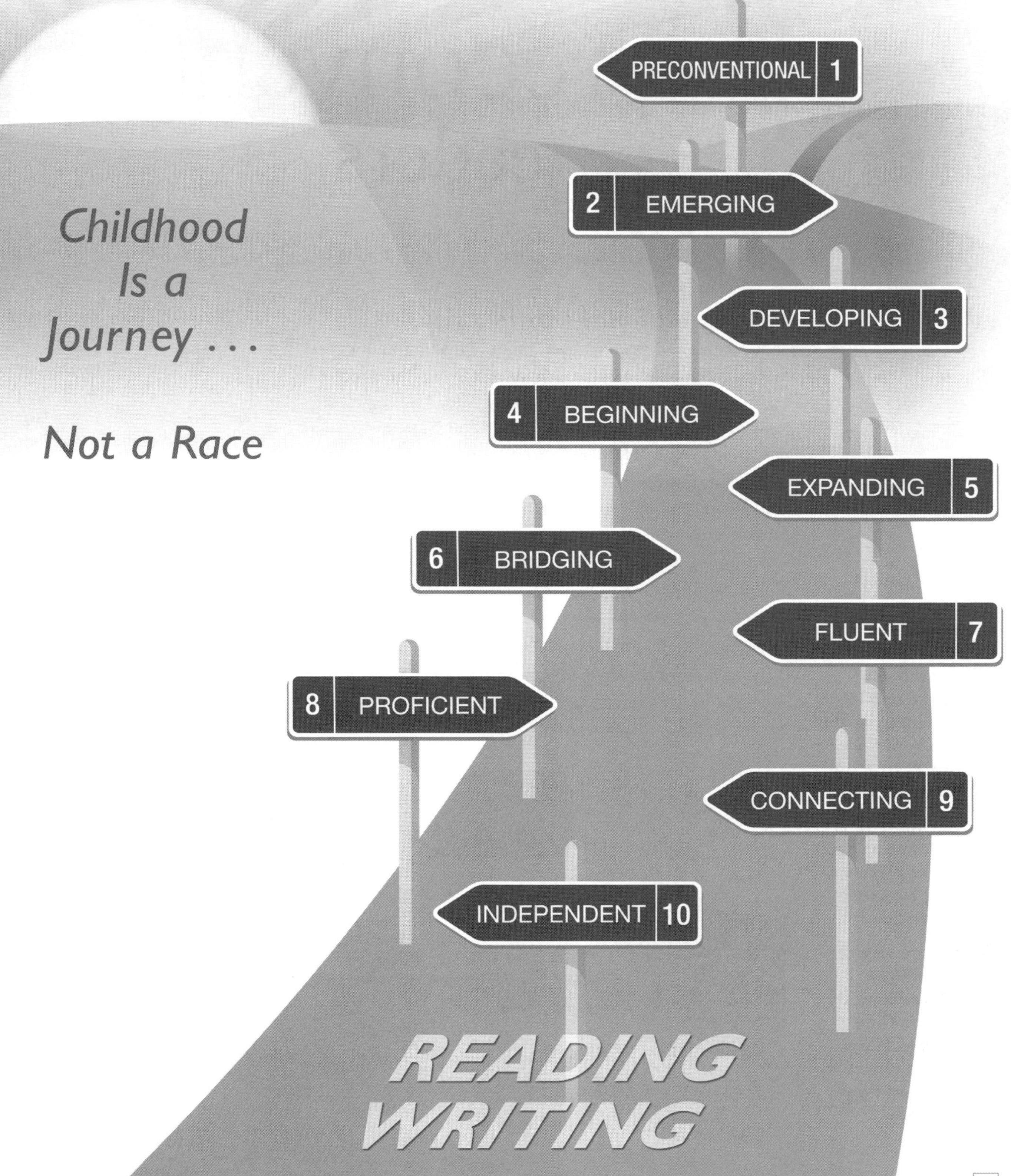

AGES 3–5

Preconventional Readers

Preconventional learners display curiosity about books and reading. They enjoy listening to books and may have favorites. Children focus mostly on illustrations at this stage as they talk about the story. They love songs and books with rhythm, repetition, and rhyme. Students participate in reading by chiming in when adults read aloud, and children at this age often enjoy hearing the same stories read aloud over and over. Preconventional readers are interested in environmental print, such as restaurant and traffic signs, labels, and logos. Children hold books correctly, turning the pages as they look at the illustrations. They know some letter names and can read and write their first name.

Preconventional readers will begin reading simple books like this one. At this stage, children will be focusing primarily on the illustrations.

PARENT tips

- ✓ **Read books with appealing pictures that match your child's age and interests. Children at this age like books with rhythm, rhyme, and repetition.**
- ✓ **Answer questions and talk about the story and pictures. Reading together should be fun!**
- ✓ **Encourage risk taking as children learn to read and memorize their first books. Have your child chime in on repeated lines or a chorus.**

Types of Texts and Oral Reading

- Begins to choose reading materials (e.g., books, magazines, and charts) and has favorites.
- Shows interest in reading signs, labels, and logos (environmental print).
- Recognizes own name in print.

Reading Strategies

- Holds book and turns pages correctly.
- Shows beginning and end of book or story.
- Knows some letter names.

Comprehension and Response

- Listens and responds to literature.
- Comments on illustrations in books.
- Participates in group reading (books, rhymes, poems, and songs).

Preconventional
Writers

At the Preconventional stage, children rely on their pictures to show meaning. They often pretend to write by using scribble writing. Children sometimes make random letters and numbers to represent words. Some children add "words" to their pictures to share meaning. They often tell stories about their pictures.

Notice the random letters that accompany this drawing.

Types of Texts

- Relies primarily on own pictures to convey meaning.
- Begins to label and add "words" to pictures.
- Writes first name.

Content and Traits

- Demonstrates awareness that print conveys meaning.

Mechanics and Conventions

- Makes marks other than drawing on paper (scribbles).
- Writes random recognizable letters to represent words.

Attitude and Self-Evaluation

- Tells about own pictures and writing.

PARENT tips

- **Provide writing materials (such as paper, pens, chalkboard or whiteboard, markers) and a corner or area for writing. You might want to have a writing box with paper, markers, and crayons in one convenient place.**
- **Model everyday writing (such as grocery lists, letters, and notes). Ask your child to add a word or picture.**
- **Play with language by singing songs, playing with rhyming words, pointing out signs, and talking about letters and words.**

Emerging Readers

At the Emerging stage, children are curious about print and see themselves as potential readers. They may pretend to read familiar poems and books. Children rely on the illustrations to tell a story but are beginning to focus on the print. They participate in readings of familiar books and often begin to memorize favorites, like *Brown Bear, Brown Bear, What Do You See?* by Bill Martin, Jr. (1967). Children begin to make connections between books read aloud and their own lives and experiences. They enjoy rhyming and playing with words. Emerging readers know most letter names and some letter sounds. They recognize some names, signs, and familiar words. These children are often highly motivated to learn to read and may move through this stage quickly.

Emerging readers will read simple books like this one with a pattern.

Types of Texts and Oral Reading

- Memorizes pattern books, poems, and familiar books.
- Begins to read signs, labels, and logos (environmental print).

Attitude

- Demonstrates eagerness to read.

Reading Strategies

- Pretends to read.
- Uses illustrations to tell stories.
- Reads top to bottom, left to right, and front to back with guidance.
- Knows most letter names and some letter sounds.
- Recognizes some names and words in context.
- Makes meaningful predictions with guidance.

Comprehension and Response

- Rhymes and plays with words.
- Participates in reading of familiar books and poems.
- Connects books read aloud to own experiences with guidance.

PARENT tips

- ✓ **Check out books on tape or CD from the library. Listen to them at bedtime or in the car.**
- ✓ **Dads, be sure to read to children, too!**
- ✓ **Write notes to your child (in his or her lunchbox, on the bed, on the mirror, or under the pillow) using simple words.**

AGES 4–6

Emerging Writers

Children at this stage begin to see themselves as writers. Some students begin to label their pictures with a few letters. They may write their name and some familiar words in a way that others can read. Students may write just the beginning or the beginning and ending sounds they hear. At the Emerging stage, children often write everything in uppercase letters. They may pretend to read their own writing, often elaborating to embellish their stories.

This student uses invented spelling to write: I went swimming at Bali.

PARENT tips

- **Keep a family calendar where you and your child can write down upcoming events and things to remember.**
- **Support invented spelling and ask children to write the sounds they hear so that they are actively figuring out how English works.**
- **Create a message center with a bulletin board or slots for mail. Encourage your child to write notes to members of the family.**

Types of Texts

- Uses pictures and print to convey meaning.
- Writes words to describe or support pictures.
- Copies signs, labels, names, and words (environmental print).

Content and Traits

- Demonstrates understanding of letter-sound relationship.

Mechanics and Conventions

- Prints with uppercase letters.
- Matches letters to sounds.
- Uses beginning consonants to make words.
- Uses beginning and ending consonants to make words.

Attitude and Self-Evaluation

- Pretends to read own writing.
- Sees self as writer.
- Takes risks with writing.

Developing Readers

Children at this stage see themselves as readers. They can read books with simple patterns, like *Dear Zoo* (Rod Campbell, 1982) or *Mrs. Wishy-Washy* (Joy Cowley, 1999), or simple texts, like *Go, Dog, Go!* (P. D. Eastman, 1961). Later in this stage, they can read books with patterns that vary more, like *Just for You* (Mercer Mayer, 1975) or *Cookie's Week* (Cindy Ward, 1988). They begin to look at books independently for short periods of time (five to ten minutes) and like to share books with others.

Developing readers know most letter sounds and can read simple words (such as *dog* and *me*) and a few sight words (such as *have* and *love*). Recognizing patterns and word families helps readers generalize what they know about one word to similar new words. They use both print and illustrations to make meaning as they read. Children often read aloud word by word, particularly with a new text. They gain fluency with familiar books and repeated readings. These young readers can retell the main idea of a story and participate in whole-group discussions of literature. This is another stage that children may pass through quickly.

Developing readers will read stories like this one with a short amount of text and the support of illustrations.

PARENT tips

- ✓ **Read different things aloud in addition to stories (such as recipes, letters, and directions).**
- ✓ **If English is not your first language, be sure to keep reading, writing, and talking together in your native language. This will help with your child's vocabulary and understanding of concepts.**
- ✓ **As you read together, ask your child to predict what might happen next or talk about how the book relates to your child's life.**

Types of Texts and Oral Reading

- Reads books with simple patterns.
- Begins to read own writing.

Attitude

- Begins to read independently for short periods (five to ten minutes).
- Discusses favorite reading material with others.

Reading Strategies

- Relies on illustrations and print.
- Uses finger-print-voice matching.
- Knows most letter sounds and letter clusters.
- Recognizes simple words.
- Uses growing awareness of sound segments (e.g., phonemes, syllables, rhymes) to read words.
- Begins to make meaningful predictions.
- Identifies titles and authors in literature (text features).

Comprehension and Response

- Retells main event or idea in literature.
- Participates in guided literature discussions.

Self-Evaluation

- Sees self as reader.
- Explains why literature is liked or disliked during class discussions with guidance.

AGES 5–7

Developing Writers

Students at the Developing stage write names and familiar words. They begin to write several short sentences about a topic. Developing writers sometimes use beginning, middle, and ending sounds to make words. For example, *learn* might be written *LRn*. This developmental reliance on the sounds of letters is called *invented spelling, phonetic spelling,* or *temporary spelling.* At this stage, students spell some high-frequency words correctly. Students often interchange upper- and lowercase letters and experiment with capital letters and simple punctuation. They write from left to right and begin to include spacing. Students are able to read their own compositions aloud immediately after writing, but later may not remember what they wrote.

This emergent writer uses conventional and phonetic spelling to write this page about clouds.

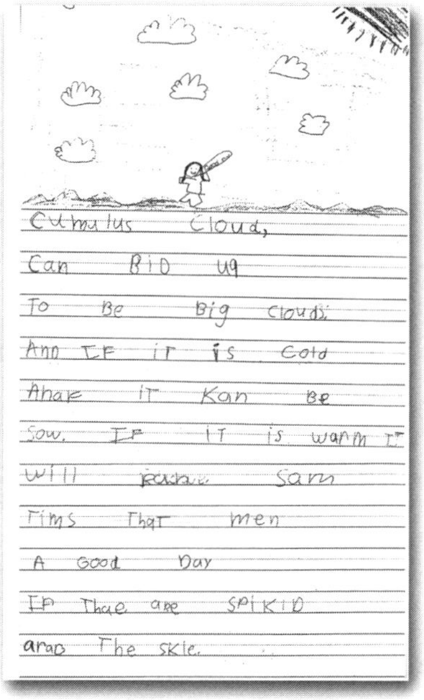

Cumulus clouds can build up to be big clouds.

And if it is cold enough it can be snow. If it is warm, it will rain. Sometimes that means a good day if they are sprinkled around the sky.

PARENT tips

Involve your child in writing party invitations, name tags, thank-you notes, valentines, holiday cards, and so on. Be sure to plan ahead enough so your child will have lots of time.

Have your children send friends post-cards when you're on a trip. Be sure to take stamps and their addresses with you.

Keep a family journal of favorite books, movies, restaurants, or jokes. Ask your child to add comments or reactions.

Types of Texts

- Writes two to four sentences about a topic.
- Writes names and familiar words.

Content and Traits

- Generates own ideas for writing.

Mechanics and Conventions

- Writes from top to bottom, left to right, and front to back.
- Intermixes uppercase and lowercase letters.
- Experiments with capitals.
- Experiments with punctuation.
- Begins to use spacing between words.
- Uses growing awareness of sound segments (e.g., phonemes, syllables, rhymes) to write words.
- Spells words on the basis of sounds without regard for conventional spelling patterns.
- Uses beginning, middle, and ending sounds to make words.

Attitude and Self-Evaluation

- Begins to read own writing.

AGES 6–8

Beginning Readers

Beginning readers rely more on print than on illustrations to create meaning. When they read aloud, they understand basic punctuation, such as periods, question marks, and exclamation marks. At first, they read simple early readers, like *The Napping House* (Audrey Wood, 1984). Students take a big step forward when they learn to read longer books, like *The Cat in the Hat* (1957) or *Green Eggs and Ham* (1960) by Dr. Seuss.

Later in this stage, they can read more difficult early readers, such as *Frog and Toad Together* (Arnold Lobel, 1971) and more challenging picture books, such as *A Bargain for Frances* (Russell Hoban, 1970). They often enjoy simple series books, such as the Little Bear books by Else Minarik or the humorous Commander Toad series by Jane Yolen. Many of these books are labeled "I Can Read" books on the covers. Beginning readers take a developmental leap as they begin to integrate reading strategies (meaning, sentence structure, and phonics cues). They are able to read silently for ten to fifteen minutes. These children know many sight words and occasionally self-correct when their reading doesn't make sense. They are able to discuss the characters and events in a story with an adult's help. When they read simple nonfiction texts, such as *Mighty Spiders* (Fay Robinson, 1996) or *Dancing with Manatees* (Faith McNulty, 1994), they are able to talk about what they learn. It may take significantly longer for children to move through this stage since there is a wide range of text complexity at this level.

Beginning readers who are in the later part of this stage will read books like this one with simple vocabulary and illustrations on every page or two.

PARENT tips

- ✓ **Begin to read series books. If you read a few, children will often read the rest of the series on their own.**
- ✓ **After you have finished a story, talk about the events and characters.**
- ✓ **Point out ways to figure out words in addition to sounding it out (such as looking at the picture, breaking the word into smaller words, reading on, or thinking about what would make sense).**

Types of Texts and Oral Reading

- Reads simple early reader books.
- Reads harder early reader books.
- Reads and follows simple written directions with guidance.
- Identifies basic genres (e.g., fiction, nonfiction, and poetry).
- Uses basic punctuation when reading orally.

Attitude

- Reads independently (ten to fifteen minutes).
- Chooses reading materials independently.
- Learns and shares information from reading.

Reading Strategies

- Uses meaning cues (context).
- Uses sentence cues (grammar).
- Uses letter-sound cues and patterns (phonics).
- Recognizes word endings, common contractions, and many high-frequency words.
- Begins to self-correct.

Comprehension and Response

- Retells beginning, middle, and end with guidance.
- Discusses characters and story events with guidance.

Self-Evaluation

- Identifies own reading behaviors with guidance.

AGES 6–8

Beginning Writers

At the Beginning stage, children write recognizable short sentences with some descriptive words. They can write one to two full pages about their lives and experiences or simple facts about a topic. Students sometimes use capitals and periods correctly. Many letters are formed legibly and adults can usually read what the child has written. Students spell some words phonetically and others are spelled correctly. They usually spell simple words and some high-frequency words correctly as they become more aware of spelling patterns. Beginning writers often start a story with "Once upon a time" and finish with "The End." Children may revise by adding details with an adult's help. They enjoy sharing their writing with others. Students may stay at this stage longer than the previous ones as they build fluency.

This beginning writer uses conventional and phonetic spelling to write these two full pages about a field trip walk along a stream.

Stream Walk
I went to a Stream Walk
with my techer and classm
We saw red ants with
there buts sticking up.
at the staiers.Then Ms.Bel
has to help us get dowr
to the water becaues
the wall was little bit
high and a little dangras.
Then all the kids includin
me has to put there
clipbord on the down in dri
rack. I saw little insecb in

the water there were
water spiders simming and
anther insect that I
don't know but it looks
like a srcot and two
legs simming in the
brown water.And anther
insect that I also don't
recnis But it looks like
an olvot sez and the
color was brown it
was hiding in a
af.

PARENT tips

- ✓ **If you have a computer, encourage your child to email friends and relatives.**
- ✓ **Have your child read you what he or she has written. Respond first to the content and ideas. At this stage, a child's confidence and attitude about writing are very important.**
- ✓ **Play word games such as *Junior Scrabble* or *Hangman*.**

Types of Texts
- Writes one to two full pages about a topic.
- Writes about observations and experiences.
- Writes short nonfiction pieces (simple facts about a topic) with guidance.

Content and Traits
- Chooses own writing topics.

Process
- Reads own writing and notices mistakes with guidance.
- Revises by adding details with guidance.

Mechanics and Conventions
- Uses spacing between words consistently.
- Forms most letters legibly.
- Writes pieces that self and others can read.
- Uses phonetic spelling to write independently.
- Spells simple words and some high-frequency words correctly.
- Begins to use periods and capital letters correctly.

Attitude and Self-Evaluation
- Shares own writing with others.

AGES 7–9

Expanding Readers

At the Expanding stage, students solidify skills as they read beginning chapter books. Many children read series books and reread old favorites while stretching into new types of reading. In the early part of this stage, they may read short series books, like Pee Wee Scouts (Judy Delton) or Pinky and Rex (James Howe). As they build fluency, students often devour series books, like Cam Jansen (David Adler), Bailey School Kids (Debbie Dadey and Marcia Thornton Jones), or Amber Brown (Paula Danziger). They may also read nonfiction texts on a topic, such as *Pompeii . . . Buried Alive!* (Edith Kunhardt, 1987). Students are learning how to choose books at their reading level and can read silently for fifteen to thirty minutes. They read aloud fluently and begin to self-correct when they make mistakes or their reading doesn't make sense. They can usually figure out difficult words but are still building their reading vocabulary. At this stage, children use a variety of reading strategies independently. These students make connections between reading and writing and their own experiences. Expanding readers are able to compare characters and events from different stories. They can talk about their own reading strategies and set goals with an adult's help.

Expanding readers often enjoy short series books like this one with familiar plots and characters.

PARENT tips

- ✓ **Read and compare several versions of a story (such as a fairy tale or folktale).**
- ✓ **Subscribe to a magazine or check magazines out from the library.**
- ✓ **Encourage your child to practice reading aloud to siblings, relatives, or senior citizens.**

Types of Texts and Oral Reading

- Reads easy chapter books.
- Chooses, reads, and finishes a variety of materials at appropriate level with guidance.
- Begins to read aloud with fluency.

Attitude

- Reads silently for increasingly longer periods (fifteen to thirty minutes).

Reading Strategies

- Uses reading strategies appropriately, depending on the text and purpose.
- Uses word structure cues (e.g., root words, prefixes, suffixes, word chunks) when encountering unknown words.
- Increases vocabulary by using meaning cues (context).
- Self-corrects for meaning.
- Follows written directions.
- Identifies chapter titles and table of contents (text organizers).

Comprehension and Response

- Summarizes and retells story events in sequential order.
- Responds to and makes personal connections with facts, characters, and situations in literature.
- Compares and contrasts characters and story events.
- "Reads between the lines" with guidance.

Self-Evaluation

- Identifies own reading strategies and sets goals with guidance.

Expanding Writers

Students at this stage can write poems and stories about their experiences and interests, as well as short nonfiction pieces. They use complete sentences and their writing contains a logical flow of ideas. Their stories sometimes contain a beginning, a middle, and an end. Expanding writers can add description, detail, and interesting language with the teacher's guidance. They enjoy reading their writing aloud and are able to offer specific feedback to other students. Their editing skills begin to grow, although students may still need help as they edit for simple punctuation, spelling, and grammar. Their writing is legible, and they no longer labor over the physical act of writing. Students spell many common words correctly as they begin to grasp spelling patterns and rules.

This student at the Expanding stage wrote a three-page booklet. Notice her use of punctuation, dialogue, and that she edited her own writing.

Name: Nitya Date: 9/14/06 Title: Going Away Party Page: 1

One evening my dad told me we were going to move. I froze... I almost cried. I tried to say "We can't move". But just as I was going to say that he interupted me and said "We have to move", everyone was quiet... then I said "Why"? becuse my job is there dad said. But dad said Disney Land was there. I felt a little better when he said that. My mother was there and was listening to our conversation. she already new we were

PARENT tips

- ✓ **Provide empty notebooks or blank books to use as journals or diaries.**
- ✓ **Make books together about trips, events, holidays, and your family.**
- ✓ **Focus on content first. Be a supportive audience for your child's writing.**

Types of Texts

- Writes short fiction and poetry with guidance.
- Writes a variety of short nonfiction pieces (e.g., facts about a topic, letters, lists) with guidance.

Content and Traits

- Writes with a central idea.
- Writes using complete sentences.
- Organizes ideas in a logical sequence in fiction and nonfiction writing with guidance.
- Begins to recognize and use interesting language.

Process

- Uses several prewriting strategies (e.g., web, brainstorm) with guidance.
- Listens to others' writing and offers feedback.
- Begins to consider suggestions from others about own writing.
- Adds description and detail with guidance.
- Edits for capitals and punctuation with guidance.
- Publishes own writing with guidance.

Mechanics and Conventions

- Writes legibly.
- Spells most high-frequency words correctly and moves toward conventional spelling.

Attitude and Self-Evaluation

- Identifies own writing strategies and sets goals with guidance.

Bridging Readers

This is a stage of consolidation when students strengthen their skills by reading longer books with more complex plots, characters, and vocabulary. They often choose well-known children's books, such as the Ramona books (Beverly Cleary) or the Encyclopedia Brown series (Donald Sobol). Students also enjoy more recent series, like Goosebumps (R. L. Stine), Animorphs (K. A. Applegate), and the Baby-sitters Club (Ann Martin). They may broaden their interests by reading a wider variety of materials, such as *Storyworks, Contact for Kids,* or *Sports Illustrated for Kids* magazines, or The Magic School Bus (Joanna Cole) nonfiction series. They begin to read aloud with expression and often memorize some of the humorous poetry by Shel Silverstein and Jack Prelutsky. With adult guidance, readers at the Bridging stage can use resources, such as encyclopedias and the Internet, to find information. They can respond to issues and ideas in books, as well as facts and story events. Many students are able to make connections between their reading and other books and authors. Students at this stage begin to support their opinions with reasons and examples during small-group literature discussions.

Chapter 1

Before Breakfast

"WHERE'S Papa going with that ax?" said Fern to her mother as they were setting the table for breakfast.

"Out to the hoghouse," replied Mrs. Arable. "Some pigs were born last night."

"I don't see why he needs an ax," continued Fern, who was only eight.

"Well," said her mother, "one of the pigs is a runt. It's very small and weak, and it will never amount to anything. So your father has decided to do away with it."

"Do *away* with it?" shrieked Fern. "You mean *kill* it? Just because it's smaller than the others?"

Mrs. Arable put a pitcher of cream on the table. "Don't yell, Fern!" she said. "Your father is right. The pig would probably die anyway."

Fern pushed a chair out of the way and ran outdoors. The grass was wet and the earth smelled of springtime. Fern's sneakers were sopping by the time she caught up with her father.

Types of Texts and Oral Reading

- Reads medium level chapter books.
- Chooses reading materials at appropriate level.
- Expands knowledge of different genres (e.g., realistic fiction, historical fiction, and fantasy).
- Reads aloud with expression.

Reading Strategies

- Uses resources (e.g., encyclopedias, CD-ROMs, and nonfiction texts) to locate and sort information with guidance.
- Gathers information by using the table of contents, captions, glossary, and index (text organizers) with guidance.
- Gathers and uses information from graphs, charts, tables, and maps with guidance.
- Increases vocabulary by using context cues, other reading strategies, and resources (e.g., dictionary and thesaurus) with guidance.
- Demonstrates understanding of the difference between fact and opinion.
- Follows multistep written directions independently.

Comprehension and Response

- Discusses setting, plot, characters, and point of view (literary elements) with guidance.
- Responds to issues and ideas in literature as well as facts or story events.
- Makes connections to other authors, books, and perspectives.
- Participates in small-group literature discussions with guidance.
- Uses reasons and examples to support ideas and opinions with guidance.

PARENT tips

- ✓ **Encourage your child to try new genres of reading (poetry, fantasy, historical fiction, and nonfiction).**
- ✓ **Keep reading aloud to your child. You can model a love of reading and fluency.**
- ✓ **When your child asks questions, seek answers together in books, encyclopedias, the newspaper, or on the Internet.**

Bridging Writers

Bridging writers begin to develop and organize their ideas into paragraphs. Students at this stage are able to write about their feelings and opinions, as well as fiction, poetry, and nonfiction. However, this is a time of practice and their writing is often uneven. Writers may focus on one aspect of a piece and pay less attention to others. For example, a student may focus on strong verbs and descriptive language, while conventions and organization move to the back burner. Students still require a great deal of adult modeling and guidance at this stage. Bridging writers are learning that meaning can be made more precise by using description, details, and interesting language. Students experiment with dialogue in their writing. They are able to edit for spelling, punctuation, and grammar. They also experiment with different types of writing as they compose longer pieces in various genres. Bridging writers use the writing process to revise, edit, and publish their work with adult support.

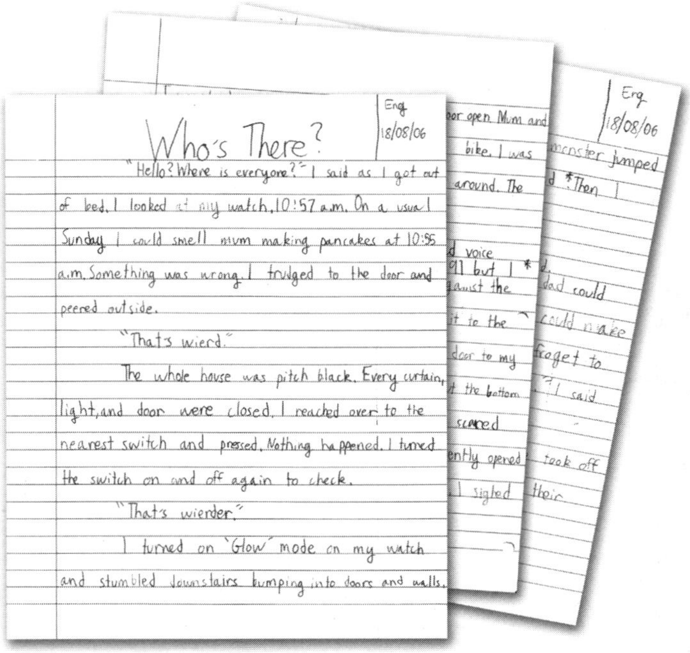

PARENT tips

✓ **On final drafts, help your child revise for meaning first. Editing for spelling and punctuation comes after revision. (A secretary can edit, but rarely revises!). Leave the pencil in your child's hands.**

✓ **Help with a few skills at a time so that revision doesn't become overwhelming. Revision and editing are challenging for young writers.**

Types of Texts

- Writes about feelings and opinions.
- Writes fiction with clear beginning, middle, and end.
- Writes poetry using carefully chosen language with guidance.
- Writes organized nonfiction pieces (e.g., reports, letters, and lists) with guidance.

Content and Traits

- Begins to use paragraphs to organize ideas.
- Uses strong verbs, interesting language, and dialogue with guidance.

Process

- Seeks feedback on writing.
- Revises for clarity with guidance.
- Revises to enhance ideas by adding description and detail.
- Uses resources (e.g., thesaurus and word lists) to make writing more effective with guidance.
- Edits for punctuation, spelling, and grammar.
- Publishes writing in polished format with guidance.

Conventions

- Increases use of visual strategies, spelling rules, and knowledge of word parts to spell correctly.
- Uses commas and apostrophes correctly with guidance.

Attitude and Self-Evaluation

- Uses criteria for effective writing to set own writing goals with guidance.

Fluent Readers

Students are well launched as independent readers by the Fluent stage. They choose to read a variety of challenging children's literature for longer periods of time (thirty to forty minutes). The books they choose have fully developed characters and challenging plots. They enjoy reading survival stories like *Hatchet* (Gary Paulsen, 1987) or *On the Far Side of the Mountain* (Jean Craighead George, 1990). Some children prefer fantasy books, such as *James and the Giant Peach* (Roald Dahl, 1961), or mystery series like Nancy Drew (Carolyn Keene) or The Hardy Boys (Franklin Dixon). Many readers at the Fluent stage enjoy magazines like *National Geographic Kids, American Girl,* or *Time for Kids.* Students are able to use resources, such as the dictionary and thesaurus. They also use the Internet and websites to find information. At this stage, children contribute thoughtful responses when they talk or write about books. Their comprehension reaches a new level when they "read between the lines" to get at deeper levels of meaning. They are learning to evaluate their own reading strategies and are able to set goals.

He rolled on his back and felt his sides and his legs, moving things slowly. He rubbed his arms; nothing seemed to be shattered or even sprained all that badly. When he was nine he had plowed his small dirt bike into a parked car and broken his ankle, had to wear a cast for eight weeks, and there was nothing now like that. Nothing broken. Just battered around a bit.

His forehead felt massively swollen to the touch, almost like a mound out over his eyes, and it was so tender that when his fingers grazed it he nearly cried. But there was nothing he could do about it and, like the rest of him, it seemed to be bruised more than broken.

I'm alive, he thought. I'm alive. It could have been different. There could have been death. I could have been done.

Like the pilot, he thought suddenly. The pilot in the plane, down into the water, down into the blue water strapped in the seat . . .

He sat up—or tried to. The first time he fell back. But on the second attempt, grunting with the effort, he managed to come to a sitting position and scrunched sideways until his back was against a small tree where he sat facing the lake, watching the sky get lighter and lighter with the coming dawn.

35

PARENT tips

- ✓ **Read book reviews in newspapers, magazines, and on the Internet. Look for the books in the library or bookstore. Give books as gifts.**
- ✓ **Talk about interesting words you find as you read. Look up the meanings together in the dictionary or online.**

Types of Texts and Oral Reading

- Reads challenging children's books.
- Selects, reads, and finishes a wide variety of genres with guidance.
- Begins to develop strategies and criteria for selecting reading materials.
- Reads aloud with fluency, expression, and confidence.

Reading Attitude

- Reads silently for extended periods (thirty to forty minutes).

Reading Strategies

- Begins to use resources (e.g., encyclopedias, articles, Internet, and nonfiction texts) to locate information.
- Gathers information by using the table of contents, captions, glossary, and index (text organizers) independently.
- Begins to use resources (e.g., dictionary and thesaurus) to increase vocabulary in different subject areas.

Comprehension and Response

- Begins to discuss literature with reference to setting, plot, characters, and theme (literary elements) and author's craft.
- Generates thoughtful oral and written responses in small-group literature discussions with guidance.
- Begins to use new vocabulary in different subjects and in oral and written response to literature.
- Begins to gain deeper meaning by "reading between the lines."

Attitude and Self-Evaluation

- Begins to set goals and identifies strategies to improve reading.

Fluent Writers

The Fluent stage is increasingly complex. Students begin to write organized fiction and nonfiction pieces for different purposes and audiences. They write stories with multiple characters, problems, and solutions with adult support. They experiment with leads, endings, and complex sentence structures. Students begin to revise for specific writing traits, such as organization or word choice. Fluent writers are able to edit for punctuation, grammar, and spelling independently. Students at this stage enjoy writing poetry with carefully chosen language. They begin to talk about the qualities of good writing in different genres. At this level, students begin to read like writers and experiment with different styles and forms of writing.

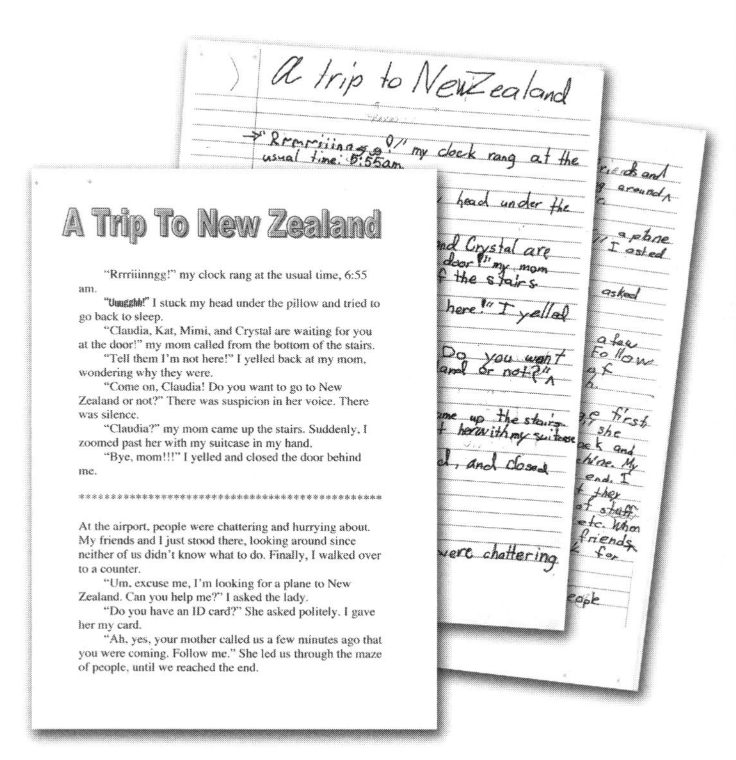

A Trip To New Zealand

"Rrrriiinngg!" my clock rang at the usual time, 6:55 am.

"Uungghh!" I stuck my head under the pillow and tried to go back to sleep.

"Claudia, Kat, Mimi, and Crystal are waiting for you at the door!" my mom called from the bottom of the stairs.

"Tell them I'm not here!" I yelled back at my mom, wondering why they were.

"Come on, Claudia! Do you want to go to New Zealand or not?" There was suspicion in her voice. There was silence.

"Claudia?" my mom came up the stairs. Suddenly, I zoomed past her with my suitcase in my hand.

"Bye, mom!!!" I yelled and closed the door behind me.

****

At the airport, people were chattering and hurrying about. My friends and I just stood there, looking around since neither of us didn't know what to do. Finally, I walked over to a counter.

"Um, excuse me, I'm looking for a plane to New Zealand. Can you help me?" I asked the lady.

"Do you have an ID card?" She asked politely. I gave her my card.

"Ah, yes, your mother called us a few minutes ago that you were coming. Follow me." She led us through the maze of people, until we reached the end.

PARENT tips

- ✓ **Help your child revise for only one thing. You can help edit when asked for assistance.**
- ✓ **Encourage your child to share finished writing with friends and relatives and to talk about his or her writing process. Encourage your child to enter a writing contest.**

Types of Texts

- Begins to write organized fiction and nonfiction (e.g., reports, letters, biographies, and autobiographies).
- Develops stories with plots that include problems and solutions with guidance.
- Creates characters in stories with guidance.
- Writes poetry using carefully chosen language.

Content and Traits

- Begins to experiment with sentence length and complex sentence structure.
- Varies leads and endings with guidance.
- Uses description, details, and similes with guidance.
- Uses dialogue with guidance.

Process

- Uses a range of strategies for planning writing.
- Adapts writing for purpose and audience with guidance.
- Revises for specific writing traits (e.g., ideas, organization, word choice, sentence fluency, voice, and conventions) with guidance.
- Incorporates suggestions from others about own writing with guidance.
- Edits for punctuation, spelling, and grammar with greater precision.
- Uses tools (e.g., dictionaries, word lists, and spell checkers) to edit with guidance.

Attitude and Self-Evaluation

- Develops criteria for effective writing in different genres with guidance.

Proficient Readers

Proficient readers seek out complex children's literature and can choose books to read independently. They read a variety of genres, such as realistic fiction, historical fiction, biographies, nonfiction, and poetry. These books are sometimes set in other countries and time periods. Novels often deal with complex issues, such as survival (*Island of the Blue Dolphins* by Scott O'Dell, 1960), death (*Bridge to Terabithia* by Katherine Paterson, 1977), or war (*Number the Stars* by Lois Lowry, 1989). Students are able to talk about the theme, author's purpose, style, and craft. Proficient readers begin to write and talk about literature at a deeper level and use reasons and examples to support their opinions. They delve into topics by reading both fiction and nonfiction materials and can locate information on a topic using several resources independently. Some students at this level enjoy challenging magazines, such as *Zillions: Consumer Reports for Kids.*

166 / *Maniac Magee*

Mars Bar wrenched free and stomped on ahead. Maniac followed. It was almost dark. High above, the streetlights were buzzing on, one by one.

After several blocks, Mars Bar wheeled. "You suckered me. You soften me up with them Pick-peoples, then bring me here. Wha'd you think? I was gonna *cry?* Okay, I come over. I did it. It's done. And don't you be comin' 'round no more, ya hear me, fish? 'Cause you ain't only seen me *half* bad yet."

He turned and headed due east. Maniac walked another way.

It was a good question. What *had* he thought? What had he expected? A miracle? Well, come to think of it, maybe one had happened. While he was looking for one miracle, maybe another had snuck up on him. It happened as he was clamping and lugging Mars Bar down the gauntlet of Cobras, trying to keep him alive — and what was Mars Bar doing? Fighting *him*, Maniac, straining to get loose and bust some Cobras. Out-numbered, out-weighed, but not out-hearted. That's when Maniac felt it — pride, for this East End warrior whom Maniac could feel trembling in his arms, scared as any normal kid would be, but not showing it to them. Yeah, you're bad all right, Mars Bar. You're more than bad. You're good.

Maniac stopped. He had been walking in circles. It was dark. He turned one way, then another, for the briefest moment thinking to go home. Thinking, it's time to go home now. Then remembering that once again he had no home to go to.

PARENT tips

- ✓ **Read the newspaper and magazines and discuss the articles together. Talk about multiple perspectives and issues in the news.**
- ✓ **Collect books by a favorite author. Research the author on the Internet. Encourage your child to write a letter to the author. Send the letter and return postage to the publisher listed near the copyright information in the front of the book.**

Types of Texts and Oral Reading

- Reads complex children's literature.
- Reads and understands informational texts (e.g., want ads, brochures, schedules, catalogs, and manuals) with guidance.
- Develops strategies and criteria for selecting reading materials independently.

Reading Strategies

- Uses resources (e.g., encyclopedias, articles, Internet, and nonfiction texts) to locate information independently.
- Gathers and analyzes information from graphs, charts, tables, and maps with guidance.
- Integrates information from multiple nonfiction sources to deepen understanding of a topic with guidance.
- Uses resources (e.g., dictionary and thesaurus) to increase vocabulary independently.

Comprehension and Response

- Identifies literary devices (e.g., similes, metaphors, personification, and foreshadowing).
- Discusses literature with reference to theme, author's purpose, style (literary elements), and craft.
- Begins to generate in-depth responses in small-group literature discussions.
- Begins to generate in-depth written response to literature.
- Uses increasingly complex vocabulary in different subjects and in oral and written response to literature.
- Uses reasons and examples to support ideas and conclusions.
- Probes for deeper meaning by "reading between the lines" in response to literature.

Proficient Writers

At the Proficient stage, students are strong writers who can write persuasively about their ideas, feelings, and opinions. Their fiction and nonfiction writing is organized, and they can weave in information from several sources with some adult guidance. They use complex sentences, sophisticated language, and imagery independently and their writing is descriptive. Proficient writers are learning how to create fiction with detailed settings and well-developed plots and characters. Students revise, edit, and publish some of their work independently. They are beginning to set their own goals and identify ways in which to improve as writers.

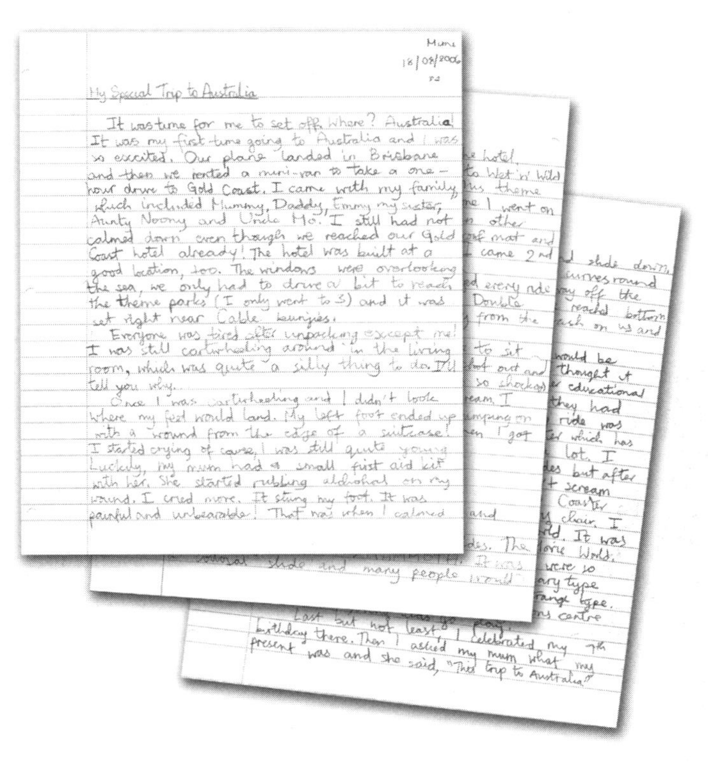
Mimi
18/08/2006

My Special Trip to Australia

It was time for me to set off. Where? Australia! It was my first time going to Australia and I was so excited. Our plane landed in Brisbane and then we rented a mini-van to take a one-hour drive to Gold Coast. I came with my family, which included Mummy, Daddy, Emmy my sister, Aunty Noony and Uncle Mo. I still had not calmed down even though we reached our Gold Coast hotel already! The hotel was built at a good location, too. The windows were overlooking the sea, we only had to drive a bit to reach the theme parks (I only went to 3) and it was set right near Cable bungies.

Everyone was tired after unpacking except me! I was still cartwheeling around in the living room, which was quite a silly thing to do. I'll tell you why.

Once I was cartwheeling and I didn't look where my feet would land. My left foot ended up with a wound from the edge of a suitcase! I started crying of course, I was still quite young. Luckily, my mum had a small first aid kit with her. She started rubbing alcohol on my wound. I cried more. It stung my foot. It was painful and unbearable! That was when I calmed

...

Last but not least, I celebrated my 7th birthday there. Then I asked my mum what my present was and she said, "The trip to Australia"

PARENT tips

- ✓ **Discuss movies and TV shows together. Talk about the writer's or director's decisions and choices. Compare the book and the movie version.**
- ✓ **Help your child to locate information in encyclopedias, nonfiction materials, and on the Internet.**

Types of Texts

- Writes persuasively about ideas, feelings, and opinions.
- Creates plots with problems and solutions.
- Begins to develop the main character and describe detailed settings.
- Begins to write organized and fluent nonfiction, including simple bibliographies.

Content and Traits

- Writes cohesive paragraphs including reasons and examples with guidance.
- Uses transitional sentences to connect paragraphs.
- Varies sentence structure, leads, and endings.
- Begins to use descriptive language, details, and similes.
- Uses voice to evoke emotional responses from readers.
- Begins to integrate information on a topic from a variety of sources.

Process

- Begins to revise for specific writing traits (e.g., ideas, organization, word choice, sentence fluency, voice, and conventions).
- Uses tools (e.g., dictionaries, word lists, spell checkers) to edit independently.
- Selects and publishes writing in polished format independently.

Conventions

- Begins to use complex punctuation (e.g., commas, colons, semicolons, and quotation marks) appropriately.

Attitude and Self-Evaluation

- Begins to set goals and identify strategies to improve writing in different genres.

Connecting
Readers

At the Connecting stage, students read both complex children's literature and young adult literature. These books include fully developed plots that often focus on complex issues, such as freedom, truth, good and evil, and human rights. Books like *Nothing but the Truth* (Avi, 1991) or *Slave Dancer* (Paula Fox, 1973) often require background knowledge and the ability to examine multiple perspectives on an issue. Many books include sophisticated language (such as the Redwall series by Brian Jacques) or complex plots (like *A Wrinkle in Time* by Madeleine L'Engle, 1962). Other books, like *The Giver* (Lois Lowry, 1993), *Wringer* (Jerry Spinelli, 1997), or *The Last Book in the Universe* (Rodman Philbrick, 2000) raise challenging issues. Characters in these novels are often approaching adolescence. Students at this stage read a variety of genres independently and are able to integrate information from fiction and nonfiction to develop a deeper understanding of a topic. They can contribute to and sustain discussions about what they read and start developing criteria for evaluating literature. They seek recommendations and opinions about books from others. Connecting readers are able to set their own reading goals and challenges independently.

Then he laughed a little. "I know it's not important, what you wear. It doesn't matter. But — "

"It's the choosing that's important, isn't it?" The Giver asked him.

Jonas nodded. "My little brother — " he began, and then corrected himself. "No, that's inaccurate. He's not my brother, not really. But this newchild that my family takes care of — his name's Gabriel?"

"Yes, I know about Gabriel."

"Well, he's right at the age where he's learning so much. He grabs toys when we hold them in front of him — my father says he's learning small-muscle control. And he's really cute."

The Giver nodded.

"But now that I can see colors, at least sometimes, I was just thinking: what if we could hold up things that were bright red, or bright yellow, and he could *choose?* Instead of the Sameness."

"He might make wrong choices."

"Oh." Jonas was silent for a minute. "Oh, I see what you mean. It wouldn't matter for a newchild's toy. But later it *does* matter, doesn't it? We don't dare to let people make choices of their own."

"Not safe?" The Giver suggested.

"Definitely not safe," Jonas said with certainty. "What if they were allowed to choose their own mate? And chose *wrong?*

"Or what if," he went on, almost laughing at the absurdity, "they chose their own *jobs?*"

"Frightening, isn't it?" The Giver said.

Jonas chuckled. "Very frightening. I can't even imagine it. We really have to protect people from wrong choices."

98

PARENT tips

- ✓ **Acknowledge your teen's or "tween's" maturing interests and help him or her find appropriate books. Don't miss the wonderful selection of young adult literature.**
- ✓ **Keep up with book reviews in newspapers, on the Internet, and at bookstores and libraries.**
- ✓ **Even if you don't have time to read together, read the books your child reads and then talk about the books together.**

Types of Texts and Oral Reading

- Reads complex children's literature and young adult literature.
- Selects, reads, and finishes a wide variety of genres independently.

Reading Attitude

- Begins to choose challenging reading materials and projects.

Reading Strategies

- Integrates nonfiction information to develop deeper understanding of a topic independently.
- Begins to gather, analyze, and use information from graphs, charts, tables, and maps.

Comprehension and Response

- Generates in-depth responses and sustains small-group literature discussions.
- Generates in-depth written responses to literature.
- Begins to evaluate, interpret, and analyze reading content critically.
- Begins to develop criteria for evaluating literature.
- Seeks recommendations and opinions about literature from others.

Attitude and Self-Evaluation

- Sets reading challenges and goals independently.

AGES 11–14

Connecting Writers

At the Connecting stage, students write in a variety of genres and forms for different purposes and audiences. Students use many different prewriting strategies to organize and strengthen their writing. They compose cohesive paragraphs, using reasons and examples for support. Connecting writers integrate information from multiple sources and create graphs and charts to convey information. They write organized, fluent, and detailed nonfiction with bibliographies using correct format. In their fiction, students create plots with a climax and believable characters. At this stage, writers use descriptive language, details, and imagery independently and may use dialogue to enhance character development. Connecting writers revise for specific writing traits (such as organization or sentence fluency) independently. As they revise, students work through several drafts independently and may rewrite or delete sections. They ask for feedback and incorporate others' suggestions into their writing.

My First Two Weeks of Middle School

As I ascended the worn stairs a huge lurch in my stomach reminded me that this was the first day of middle school. Grasping my new notebooks and pencils I quickly searched for a teacher that might help me but found no one. It was so early not even the roosters had sung their daily cock-a-doodle-doo. Running frantically frustrated to a sobbing point, it suddenly occurred to me that I was alone. After leaving so early the world seemed to simply empty itself of any living thing. And finally I ran (literally) into Carly, who was going to seventh grade this year. 15 minutes later I was sitting down patiently awaiting in front of the dark library awaiting the arrival of my synergy teacher to get me organized. Later, after school, I came back with a bundle of organization tools and got everything in my locker organized. Now I looked up to the stars with a shining light of hope for the term.

I remember the summer before middle school very well and am not going to forget it too soon. In preparation for every subject, it was very stressing to keep up with every thing going on but it proved to be very worthy. Scanning through textbooks reviewing math, reading as much as I could to strenghthen my reading skills, practicing my flute to stay in shape, and running at least a mile every day for P.E. It was comforting, but on the first day I shuddered on how I would feel if I didn't prepare. It was nice of the school to give us a practice day and meet all the teachers, but it just intensified my fears of the first real day.

Lunch was a problem. A big one. Not being used to eating with mixed grades, it was very disturbing to eat while some high schoolers behind you chatted like they needed it to breathe. For the first few days my fears overcame me and I just ate sandwhiches while wandering endlessly in the hollowed halls of ISB. But finally some friends I had in 7th grade invited me to eat with them while passing them with my usual chicken sandwich. And being deprived too long of my 5th grade friends, I finally spent a whole lunch time looking for my long lost friends. When they finally popped up, a wave of relief came thundering down on me in a pleasant way.

PARENT **tips**

- ✓ **Play word games together, such as *Boggle* or *Scrabble*.**
- ✓ **Share examples of good writing from articles or the books you read.**

Types of Texts

- Writes in a variety of genres and forms for different audiences and purposes independently.
- Creates plots with a climax.
- Creates detailed, believable settings and characters in stories.
- Writes organized, fluent, and detailed nonfiction independently, including bibliographies with correct format.

Content and Traits

- Writes cohesive paragraphs including supportive reasons and examples.
- Uses descriptive language, details, similes, and imagery to enhance ideas independently.
- Begins to use dialogue to enhance character development.
- Incorporates personal voice in writing with increasing frequency.
- Integrates information on a topic from a variety of sources independently.
- Constructs charts, graphs, and tables to convey information when appropriate.

Process

- Uses prewriting strategies effectively to organize and strengthen writing.
- Revises for specific writing traits (e.g., ideas, organization, word choice, sentence fluency, voice, and conventions) independently.
- Includes deletion in revision strategies.
- Incorporates suggestions from others on own writing independently.

Mechanics and Conventions

- Uses complex punctuation (e.g., commas, colons, semicolons, and quotation marks) with increasing accuracy.

Independent Readers

Students at this stage read both young adult and adult literature. Young adult books often focus on issues of growing up and entering adulthood. They include multiple characters who encounter complex issues and challenging obstacles. Some examples of young adult novels are *Ironman* (Chris Crutcher, 1995), *The Devil's Arithmetic* (Jane Yolen, 1988), *The Golden Compass* (Philip Pullman, 1995), *Shabanu* (Suzanne Fisher Staples, 1989), and The Lord of the Rings series by J. R. R. Tolkien. These students read a range of sophisticated materials for pleasure, to learn information, and to solve problems. For instance, they may read newspapers and magazines, download information from a website, or read longer biographies, such as *Eleanor Roosevelt* by Russell Freedman (1993). When they respond to literature during discussions or in writing, students add insightful comments as they make connections between other books and authors, their background knowledge, and their own lives. They stick with complex reading challenges and are able to evaluate and analyze what they read. Independent readers are interested in hearing other people's perspectives and sharing their opinions about what they have read.

The color softens on her skin, leaving her tiger eyes looking fiery. She wipes it away before Dadi comes home. But she'll wear it on her wedding day.

Phulan spends her days resting, eating, and sleeping, being pampered and fussed over, trying on her dowry clothes and jewelry, and talking about the sons she will have.

Half of me longs to be Phulan. She will marry my own dear Murad, and she is beautiful. I am small and strong with too much spirit, and I think too much. I am lonely and fearful, and I long for the days when I was free in the desert.

Again the man on the white horse comes, the starched pleats of his turban dazzling in the monsoon sunlight. Dadi holds the reins as the man dismounts. This time he hands Dadi a tiny sack of lambskin tied with gold threads. Dadi thanks him, and the man bows formally. Mirrors dazzling on his vest, he remounts his silver horse and rides away again.

I untie the threads, and a silver vial with vines and flowers carved over its surface slides into my palm. I open the stopper, a tiny dove perched atop a long ivory applicator, and draw out a miniature spoonful of lapis lazuli powder to decorate my own eyes.

I do resent his trying to buy my heart. Bride price is common here in the desert—I don't begrudge Mama and Dadi that. It has insured their future, and they won't have to worry about drought or anything else ever again. But my heart. I never knew I had one until I lost Guluband.

202

PARENT tips

- ✓ **Talk about the books you are reading. Share interesting passages or quotes.**
- ✓ **Subscribe to a magazine based on your child's interests. Even if you might prefer a different subject matter, it will keep your child reading at an age when reading tends to decline.**

Types of Texts and Oral Reading

- Reads young adult and adult literature.
- Chooses and comprehends a wide variety of sophisticated materials with ease (e.g., newspapers, magazines, manuals, novels, and poetry).
- Reads and understands informational texts (e.g., manuals, consumer reports, applications, and forms).

Reading Attitude

- Reads challenging materials for pleasure independently.
- Reads challenging material for information and to solve problems independently.
- Perseveres through complex reading tasks.

Reading Strategies

- Gathers, analyzes, and uses information from graphs, charts, tables, and maps independently.

Comprehension and Response

- Analyzes literary devices (e.g., metaphors, imagery, irony, and satire).
- Contributes unique insights and supports opinions in complex literature discussions.
- Adds depth to responses to literature by making insightful connections to other reading and experiences.
- Evaluates, interprets, and analyzes reading content critically.
- Develops and articulates criteria for evaluating literature.

Attitude and Self-Evaluation

- Pursues a widening community of readers independently.

Independent Writers

Writers at the Independent stage create cohesive, in-depth fiction with carefully chosen language and strong characters, setting, plot, and mood. They use dialogue and literary devices (such as metaphors and imagery) effectively. They also write accurate and fluent nonfiction on a variety of topics. Writing has become natural and they have internalized the writing process. Independent writers seek feedback from others and work on multiple drafts. They begin to develop a personal voice and style of writing. In final drafts, there are very few spelling, punctuation, or grammatical errors. Students at this stage can analyze their own writing and set goals independently. They write with confidence and competence and persevere through complex writing projects.

The Roots of Satisfaction

As natural to man as his need to eat, to breathe, as forceful as his drive to explore and learn, as passionate as his hunt for love or lust is his quest for true happiness and satisfaction. Perhaps, one might even say it is the inherent motivation for everything we do. It is our hidden agenda, our underlying motive lurking beneath the façade of even the most selfless act. But to quest for joy is by no means at all a guarantee of its attainment. Even the founding fathers of America acknowledged this by assuring not pleasure, but the *pursuit* of pleasure in the constitution of the nation. One of the keys to enjoying a life is discovering happiness and its sources and origins, be they as frivolous and fleeting as a match of tennis or as deep and ponderous as a discussion on the meaning of life. But even these joys often wane with time, leaving a vague ache in their absence, forcing us to press onward for other external sources of satisfaction. In answer to this, *Anna Karenina*, by Leo Tolstoy, establishes that true happiness stems not from without, but from within.

Throughout the epic and far-reaching tale it is illustrated clearly that to be truly satisfied requires us to find purpose within ourselves. This belief of Tolstoy's bears a distinct similarity to the concept of Dharma, a primary tenet of Hinduism which maintains that everyone has a duty and purpose in life which they must fulfill, lest they betray their own innate nature and the universe itself. Consider Levin, for example, who enjoys passionately his labors on the farm, growing crops, and his awe and wonder at the birth of his child. "Before that, if Levin had been told that Kitty was dead, and that he had died with her, that they had angel children, and that God was there present with them-he would not have been astonished." (Tolstoy, 710) This passage describing Levin's awe and mysticism at the divine influence he sees in the birth of his son

PARENT tips

✓ **Do crossword puzzles together.**

✓ **Encourage your child to take a writing or journalism class or submit writing to the school's literary magazine or a writing contest.**

Types of Texts

- Writes organized, fluent, accurate, and in-depth nonfiction, including references with correct bibliographic format.
- Writes cohesive, fluent, and effective poetry and fiction.

Content and Traits

- Uses a clear sequence of paragraphs with effective transitions.
- Begins to incorporate literary devices (e.g., imagery, metaphors, personification, and foreshadowing).
- Weaves dialogue effectively into stories.
- Develops plots, characters, setting, and mood (literary elements) effectively.
- Begins to develop personal voice and style of writing.

Process

- Revises through multiple drafts independently.
- Seeks feedback from others and incorporates suggestions in order to strengthen own writing.
- Publishes writing for different audiences and purposes in polished format independently.
- Internalizes the writing process.

Conventions

- Uses complex grammar (e.g., subject and verb agreement and verb tense) consistently.

Attitude and Self-Evaluation

- Writes with confidence and competence on a range of topics independently.
- Perseveres through complex or challenging writing projects independently.
- Sets writing goals independently by analyzing and evaluating own writing.

When we finish reading, ask me some of these questions.

Which words rhyme in the story?

◆

What happened in the story?

◆

Who are the characters in the story?

◆

What was your favorite part of the story?

◆

Tell me about the (things, places, or animals) in this story.

◆

What is the title of the story?

Emerging

When we finish reading, ask me some of these questions.

What happened at the beginning (or end) of the story?

◆

What happened in the story?

◆

Who are the characters in the story?

◆

What was your favorite part of the story?

◆

Tell me about the (things, places, or animals) in this story.

◆

How were (name two characters) alike/different from each other?

Developing

When we finish reading, ask me some of these questions.

What happened at the (beginning, middle, or end) of the story?

◆

What was the main idea of the story?

◆

Who are the characters in the story?

◆

Who was the main character? Did you like/dislike them?

◆

What was the setting?

◆

How were (name two characters) alike/different from each other?

◆

What was the problem in the story and how was it solved?

◆

Does this story remind you of something you have done or read about?

Beginning

When we finish reading, ask me some of these questions.

Retell the main events in the story in order.

◆

What was the main idea of the story?

◆

Who are the characters in the story and what are they like?

◆

Why do you think (pick a character) acted that way?

◆

What was the setting?

◆

How were (name two characters) alike/ different from each other?

◆

What was the problem in the story and how was it solved?

◆

Does this story remind you of something you have done or read about?

◆

What was the author trying to tell the reader?

Expanding

When we finish reading, ask me some of these questions.

Summarize what happened in the story.

◆

What was the main idea of the story?

◆

Who are the characters in the story and what are they like?

◆

Why do you think (pick a character) acted that way?

◆

What do you think the author's purpose was in writing this piece?

◆

How were (name two characters) alike/ different from each other?

◆

Which sentence gives the most important idea in the selection?

◆

Does this story remind you of something you have done or read about?

◆

What was the author trying to tell the reader?

Bridging

When we finish reading, ask me some of these questions.

Summarize what happened in the story.

◆

What was the main idea of the piece?

◆

Describe the characters, their traits, and how they interact with each other in this story.

◆

Why do you think (pick an event) happened that way?

◆

What do you think the author's message was in writing this piece? Do you agree with it?

◆

What problem did the character face in the piece? How did the character feel about the problem?

◆

What do you think would happen next if the book continued?

◆

What was the author trying to tell the reader?

Fluent

When we finish reading, ask me some of these questions.

Summarize what happened in the story.

◆

What was the main idea of the piece?
Which sentences support your view?

◆

Describe the characters, their traits, and how they interact with each other in this story.

◆

Find two similes or metaphors in the piece.

◆

What do you think the author's message was in writing this piece?
Do you agree with it?

◆

What problem did the character face in the piece?
How did the character feel about the problem?

◆

How would you describe this author's style?

◆

What was the author trying to tell the reader?

Proficient

When we finish reading, ask me some of these questions.

Summarize what happened in the story.

◆

What was the main idea of the piece?
Which sentences support your view?

◆

Analyze the characters, their traits, and how they interact with each other in this story.

◆

Find two similes or metaphors in the piece.

◆

Would you recommend this piece to someone else? Why?

◆

What problem did the character face in the piece? How did the character feel about the problem?

◆

How would you describe this author's style?

◆

What is the author's purpose in writing this piece?

Connecting & Independent